The Weimar Republic, 1918–29

The origins of the republic, 1918–19

1 Describe the roles of both Friedrich Ebert and Philipp Scheidemann within the new government.

....

....

....

....

2 Explain two strengths of the German Constitution.

....

....

....

....

....

3 Why was Article 48 a weakness within the constitution?

....

....

....

....

4 Arrange the following events into the correct sequence so that you end up with a timeline for the creation of the new German republic. Using arrows, place the events in the table provided below, from the earliest in the first column to the latest in the final column.

| Kaiser Wilhelm II abdicates | German naval mutiny | A coalition government is formed with Friedrich Ebert as president |
| Elections held for a Constituent Assembly | Prince Max of Baden helps form a new government | A new German republic is declared |

Earliest				Latest

5. The following key words relate to the Weimar Constitution. In the final column, insert the correct letter, linking each key word to the correct definition.

Key word	Definition	Answer
a Constitution	The German parliament	
b Coalition government	Those people eligible to vote in elections	
c Reichstag	A set of rules defining the way that a state is governed	
d Electorate	The title given to the new leader of Germany, who would propose laws and represent the nation	
e Chancellor	A form of government in which the people vote for political representatives in an election — a president, not a monarch, is usually the highest representative	
f Republic	A government formed of more than one political party	

6. Which statements are true and which are false? Circle True or False accordingly. Correct the false statements in the space provided below so that they are historically accurate.

Statement	True/False?
Men and women over the age of 18 could vote for Reichstag members.	True/False
Presidential elections were held every 7 years.	True/False
The president could use Article 48 to enact laws without the involvement of the Reichstag.	True/False
Reichstag elections were held every 6 years.	True/False
The Reichsrat could propose laws.	True/False

....
....
....
....

Exam-style questions

Section A

7. Explain why the Weimar Constitution caused problems for democracy.

You may use the following in your answer:

- Article 48
- Proportional representation

You **must** also use information of your own. If you run out of space, you may continue your answer on a separate piece of paper.

⏱ 15   **12 marks**

....
....
....
....

Section A

8 Give two points you can infer from Source A regarding the end of the First World War and its consequences for Germany. Then add the details from the source that tell you this.

⏱ 5   **4 marks**

Source A

What I can infer:

Details in the source that tell me this:

What I can infer:

Details in the source that tell me this:

Foch and the Armistice Treaty imposed on Germany, 11 November 1918 (caricature by Kirby)

The Weimar Republic, 1918–29

Early challenges to the Weimar Republic, 1919–23

9 Rank the following terms of the Treaty of Versailles in order of their effect on civilians, with 1 being the greatest effect and 5 the most minimal. There is no single answer, so you should be prepared to explain your choices in the final column.

Term	Rank (1–5)	Explanation
All colonies handed over to the allies (Great Britain and France)		
Reparations (money to pay damages)		
Army to not exceed 100,000 troops		
Germany to accept blame for initiating the First World War		
No union with Austria (known as Anschluss)		

10 Explain the stab-in-the-back theory in no more than ten words.

....

....

11 a Consider how the following left-wing and right-wing uprisings affected the Weimar Republic. Place them on the threat continuum in the table provided below, from the most extreme threat in the first column to the least threatening in the final column.

Spartacist rising, 1919 (left-wing)	Kapp Putsch, 1920 (right-wing)	Communist rising in the Ruhr, 1920 (left-wing)	Munich Putsch, 1923 (right-wing)
Most extreme			**Least extreme**

b Explain your choices for the most extreme and least extreme uprisings.

....

....

....

....

12 Summarise the role of the foreign minister Gustav Stresemann between 1923 and 1929.

....

....

....

13 State how successful the Weimar Republic was in tackling each of the following events:

a Spartacist revolt, 1919

....

....

....

b Occupation of the Ruhr, 1923

....

....

....

c Hyperinflation, 1923

....

....

....

14 Which of the following statements were causes, immediate consequences or long-term consequences of hyperinflation? Circle the answer accordingly.

Statement	Cause, immediate consequence or long-term consequence?
French and Belgian troops occupied the Rhineland in January 1923, leading to passive resistance in the Ruhr.	Cause / Immediate consequence / Long-term consequence
Loans from the USA were negotiated, allowing Germany to pay back its reparations and begin a new programme of house and road building.	Cause / Immediate consequence / Long-term consequence
The currency became worthless as more and more of it was printed. Those with savings or on a fixed income were most affected and blamed the government for the crisis.	Cause / Immediate consequence / Long-term consequence
German workers in the Ruhr went on strike over the invasion of their homeland.	Cause / Immediate consequence / Long-term consequence
The German government backed the strikers and continued to pay their wages by printing money. However, the government had to start importing coal to cover the shortfall in production.	Cause / Immediate consequence / Long-term consequence
Reparations were finally set at £6.6 billion in 1921. It was difficult for the German government to pay this amount.	Cause / Immediate consequence / Long-term consequence
As the cost of items went up and the government started to print more money, people suffered as prices soared.	Cause / Immediate consequence / Long-term consequence
In the summer of 1923 the new chancellor, Gustav Stresemann, introduced a new currency, accepted the terms of the Treaty of Versailles and sent the workers back to producing goods. This helped to stabilise the situation.	Cause / Immediate consequence / Long-term consequence

Exam-style questions

Section A

15 Give two points you can infer from Source B about the threats from the left and the right for civilians. Then add the details from the source that tell you this. **4 marks**

Source B

Street fighting in Berlin between government troops and Spartacists, 1 January 1919

What I can infer: ....

....

Details in the source that tell me this: ....

....

....

....

What I can infer: ....

....

Details in the source that tell me this: ....

....

....

....

Section A

16 Explain how large a threat the Kapp Putsch was for the Weimar Republic.

You may use the following in your answer:
- the Treaty of Versailles
- the Dolchstoss theory

You **must** also use information of your own. If you run out of space, you may continue your answer on a separate piece of paper.

⏰ 15   **12 marks**

....
....
....
....
....
....
....
....

Changes in society, 1924–29

17 a Decide whether or not the following events show that Germany was undergoing a 'golden age' in 1924–29. Explain your reasoning in the final column.

Event	Golden age (Yes/No)?	Why?
The German actress Marlene Dietrich became one of the most popular film stars in the world.		
The Weimar government relaxed censorship.		
US loans were called in after the Wall Street Crash in 1929.		
Up until 1930 the moderate Social Democrats always won the most votes in the Reichstag.		
In literature, extreme radicals from both the left and right were able to publish their views.		
Women over 20 could vote and became more involved in politics.		
In 1927, workers and organisations were required to pay into a national scheme for unemployment welfare.		
The second reparations negotiation, the Young Plan (1929), extended the period for repayment and reduced the debt by about 20%.		

The Weimar Republic, 1918–29

b Explain how far Germany was undergoing a golden age by September 1929.

....

....

....

18 The following key words relate to the notion of society. Draw a line or arrow linking each key word to an example.

Key word	Example
Employment	The filmmaker Fritz Lang helped to create a new sense of the future with his 1927 film *Metropolis*.
Politics	The German historians Arthur Moeller van den Bruck and Oswald Spengler were highly critical of German democracy.
Housing	The Reichstag issued decrees that created greater equality in education and in civil service appointments.
Leisure	The Bauhaus movement introduced an innovative and modernist style that united simplified forms with vivid colours and unusual materials.
Art	By 1933, there were 100,000 female teachers and 3,000 new doctors.
Architecture	Otto Dix, a former soldier during the First World War, created realistic depictions of the brutality of war and everyday life in the Weimar Republic.
Literature	Women could go out unescorted and drink and smoke in public.
Cinema	By 1929, the state was spending 33 times more on housing than it had been in 1913.

19 Fill in the dates and explain what happened in each event.

Event	Date	Explanation
Locarno treaties		
Kellogg-Briand Pact		
Stresemann awarded the Nobel Peace Prize		
League of Nations		
Dawes Plan		
Allied troops evacuated from the Ruhr		
Young Plan		
Wall Street Crash		

20 The following facts relate to the changes in German society. Circle the correct answers.

a Due to the increased spending on housing, by how much was homelessness reduced by 1928?

50%   60%   70%

b In 1928 real wages had risen by how much?

12%   22%   32%

c Due to increases in state spending, by 1929 the state was now spending how much more on housing than it had in 1913?

13 times   23 times   33 times

d How many female deputies were there in the Reichstag in 1926?

6   32   55

e By 1933, were there more female doctors or female teachers as a result of the Weimar Republic?

doctors   teachers

21 Between 1924 and 1929 the Weimar government helped to create a period in German history that allowed culture and society to thrive. Create a spider diagram to explain how each of the following cultural and societal strands changed during this period.

| Art | Cinema | Literature | Architecture |
| Housing | Employment | Politics | Theatre |

22 Consolidate your knowledge of the cultural changes in Weimar Germany. Using the following list of names and terms, write a paragraph summarising the changes:

- Otto Dix
- Marlene Dietrich
- golden age
- censorship
- women
- the Bauhaus movement
- freedom
- the Wall Street Crash
- future
- the First World War

....
....
....
....
....
....
....
....
....

Exam-style questions

Section B

23 Study Sources C and D. How useful are these sources for an enquiry into the recovery of the Weimar Republic between 1924 and 1929?

Explain your answer using Sources C and D and your own knowledge of the historical context. If you run out of space, you may continue on a separate piece of paper.

⏱ 10 **8 marks**

Source C

Germany has raised herself up to shoulder the terrific burden of this peace in a way we would never have thought possible. So that today after 10 years we may say with certainty 'Even so, it might have been worse'. The stage of convalescence from Versailles is a very long road to go and we have travelled it surprisingly quickly.

From a German journalist, written in 1930 (*Weimar and Nazi Germany, 1918–39*, S. Waugh & J. Wright, 2016)

Source D

However, the German recovery still had serious weaknesses. It depended on American loans which could be withdrawn at any time. Unemployment was a serious problem. The economy might be growing, but it wasn't creating jobs fast enough for Germany's rising population. Some sectors of the economy were in trouble throughout the 1920s, farming in particular.

From *A History of Germany, 1918–45* (Hodder, 2018), written in 1997 (*Weimar and Nazi Germany, 1918–39*, S. Waugh & J. Wright, 2016)

....

Section A

24 Explain how important the Young Plan was to the recovery of the German economy by 1929.

You may use the following in your answer:
- the Dawes Plan
- the Locarno treaties

You **must** also use information of your own. If you run out of space, you may continue your answer on a separate piece of paper.

15 | 12 marks

The Weimar Republic, 1918–29

Hitler's rise to power, 1919–33

Early development of the Nazi Party, 1920–28

1 Arrange the following events into the correct sequence so that you end up with a timeline for the origins of the German Workers' Party. Place the events in the table provided below, from the earliest in the first column in the top row to the latest in the final column in the bottom row.

| *Mein Kampf* is published | Hitler joins the German Workers' Party | The Munich Putsch | The Nazis win 12 seats in the Reichstag |
| Hitler introduces the Sturmabteilung (SA), otherwise known as the Brownshirts | The Wall Street Crash and the death of Gustav Stresemann | Hitler serves time in Landsberg Prison | The Bamberg Conference |

Earliest			
			Latest

2 Consider the following points from the Nazis' 25-Point Programme and how they affected the attitudes of the German electorate.

    i   The union of all Germans into a Greater Germany

    ii   The scrapping of the Treaty of Versailles

    iii Citizenship of the state to be granted to people of German blood only — no Jewish person was to be a citizen of the nation

    iv The right to vote in elections given only to German citizens

    v   Citizens entitled to a job and a decent standard of living — if this could not be achieved, foreign nationals were to be deported

    vi All citizens have equal rights and duties

    vii The government to nationalise all businesses that were formed into corporations

    viii Pensions to be improved

    ix Improved education so that all Germans could find employment

    x   Religious freedom for all — providing the views expressed did not threaten or offend the German people

a Why might points v, viii and ix appeal to many German citizens in 1923?

....

....

....

b Why do you think the Nazi party included points i and ii into their manifesto?

....

....

....

c What does point iii suggest about Nazi party policies and who they wanted to support?

....

....

....

d Why do you think votes for the Nazi party were so low in 1928, considering that they had made these claims in their 25 Point Programme?

....

....

....

3 Which statements are true and which are false? Circle True or False accordingly. Correct the false statements in the space provided below so that they are historically accurate.

Statement	True/False?
Adolf Hitler spent 5 years living on the streets and earned a living by selling his own hand-painted postcards.	True/False
Hitler fled to Munich to avoid joining the Austrian army in 1913.	True/False
During the First World War Hitler was shot, but by 1918 he was fit and well and serving on the front line.	True/False
Adolf Hitler set up the German Workers' Party in 1920.	True/False
Hitler wrote the party's manifesto in February 1922.	True/False

....

....

....

....

4 Describe the role of the SA in no more than ten words.

....

....

Hitler's rise to power, 1919–33

5 Which of the following statements were causes, immediate consequences or long-term consequences of the Munich Putsch? Circle the answer accordingly.

Statement	Cause, immediate consequence or long-term consequence?
During his trial, Hitler gained national recognition for his debating ability. This won him support from nationalists outside of Bavaria.	Cause / Immediate consequence / Long-term consequence
During his time in prison Hitler was able to gather support and backing from leading industrialists, who would later fund the Nazi campaign.	Cause / Immediate consequence / Long-term consequence
Benito Mussolini had led a seizure of power in Italy in 1922, using his private army (the Blackshirts) to march on the capital.	Cause / Immediate consequence / Long-term consequence
Hitler realised that a coup would not allow the party to gain control of Germany. He therefore changed the party's focus to winning elections.	Cause / Immediate consequence / Long-term consequence
The growth in support for the Nazi Party across southern Germany made the party more popular and therefore more powerful.	Cause / Immediate consequence / Long-term consequence
Hitler believed that leading members of the Bavarian government opposed the Weimar Republic.	Cause / Immediate consequence / Long-term consequence
Hitler was arrested and put on trial. He was found guilty and sent to prison to serve 5 years, but only served 9 months.	Cause / Immediate consequence / Long-term consequence
The Nazi Party went into decline.	Cause / Immediate consequence / Long-term consequence

6 The following measures were introduced to reorganise the Nazi Party in order to win elections. State how each method helped the party reach its goal.

Measure	How did it help the Nazi Party to win elections?
The party was restructured to include branches called Gaue.	
In order to fulfil the Führerprinzip only Hitler's closest associates would help run the party from Munich.	
At the Bamberg Conference in 1926 Hitler appointed Gregor Strasser as propaganda leader and Josef Goebbels as Gauleiter for Berlin.	
Hitler replaced Ernst Röhm with Ernst von Salomon as the leader of the SA.	
Propaganda would be used to reinforce the Nazi Party manifesto.	
Hitler changed his target audience in order to attract the rural voter, at a time when the farming industry was experiencing economic problems.	

Exam-style questions

Section B

7 Study Sources E and F. How useful are these sources for an enquiry into the actions of the SA?

Explain your answer using Sources E and F and your own knowledge of the historical context. If you run out of space, you may continue on a separate piece of paper.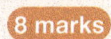

Source E

The Torchlight Procession of the SA in Berlin 30th January 1933, created by an unknown artist, 30 January 1933

Source F

[The Nazis] smashed the windows of...department stores in the Leipzigerstrasse. In the evening they assembled in the Potsdamer Platz, shouting 'Germany awake!', 'Death to Judah', 'Heil Hitler'... In the main [they] consisted of adolescent riff-raff which made off yelling as soon as the police began to use truncheons. I have never witnessed so much rabble in these parts.

Count Harry Kessler was a German diplomat who wrote about his experiences living in several European countries. This account was written Monday 13 October 1930, in Berlin.

Section B

8 a Study Interpretations 1 and 2, which provide differing views regarding the importance of the Munich Putsch. What is the main difference between these views? Explain your answer, using details from both interpretations.

4 marks

Interpretation 1

[The] coup was not even close to success. Kahr and his colleagues had escaped and were rallying forces against the coup... Ludendorff suggested a march on the town centre and Hitler, after some hesitation, agreed... Someone...fired at the police cordon and the machine guns opened fire... Hitler threw himself to the ground...and was saved from death by his bodyguard... Hitler limped away in the confusion...

From *The Third Reich: A Chronicle* (R. Overy, 2010)

Interpretation 2

The 'Hitler-Putsch' was... by no means merely Hitler's Putsch. The Bavarian Reichswehr had colluded massively in the training and preparation of the forces which had tried to take over the state. And important personages had been implicated in the Putsch attempt. Whatever their subsequent defence of their actions, the hands of Kahr, Lossow, and Seisser were dirty.

From *Hitler* (I. Kershaw, 2008)

b Suggest one reason why Interpretations 1 and 2 give different views about the importance of the Munich Putsch.

4 marks

c How far do you agree with Interpretation 2 about the importance of the Munich Putsch? Explain your answer, using both interpretations and your knowledge of the historical context.

Make notes in the space below, then write your answer on a separate piece of paper.

30 | 20 marks

The growth in support for the Nazis, 1929–32

9 In the table provided, place the following German chancellors in the correct chronological order in terms of their period in office. Add the dates of office for each of the chancellors and an explanation for why their time in office came to an end.

| Franz von Papen | Kurt von Schleicher | Heinrich Brüning |

Chancellor	Dates in office	Explanation

10 Explain why there were so many different German chancellors in such a short space of time.

11 Which of the following factors were likely to have affected a citizen's decision over whether or not to support the Nazi Party? Add the factor/s (there could be more than one) to the table and explain your reasoning.

| Fear of communism | The economic crisis of the Great Depression | Propaganda | Failed government | The Nazi Party manifesto |

Citizen	Factor(s)	Explanation
The owner of a large business who is afraid of the growth in trade unions and increase in workers' demands		
An unemployed factory worker who is struggling to pay his rent and provide for his family due to a lack of government support		
A young student who has joined the Nazi Party in hopes of securing a job		
A woman afraid of the gangs of workers patrolling the streets in support of the communists		
A farmer who is disgruntled by the reduction in pension payments and the fall in food prices		

12 Put these events in chronological order by writing one of the numbers 1–10 in the empty column, with 1 being the earliest and 10 the latest.

Event	Chronological order (1–10)
Heinrich Brüning had to rely on President Hindenburg and Article 48 because he did not receive a majority in the Reichstag.	
Franz von Papen was the next chancellor. He called an election in July 1932. The Nazis won 230 seats, making them, for the first time, the largest party in the Reichstag.	
Von Papen of the Centre Party refused to resign and Hitler demanded the job of chancellor for himself.	
When von Papen failed to secure another majority and with Hitler still requesting the job of chancellor, Hindenburg turned to the defence minister, Kurt von Schleicher, to create a cross-party alliance.	
Chancellor Hermann Müller failed to deal with the economic crisis after the Wall Street Crash, and Heinrich Brüning replaced him. A general election was called in September 1930, with Brüning hopeful of a win that would allow him to rule without Hindenburg's help.	
To block Schleicher and try to maintain power, von Papen turned to Hitler to make a political deal. He would be vice-chancellor to Hitler's chancellor.	
The Nazis won 107 seats, making them the second-largest party after the Social Democrats with 143 seats.	
Several German banks collapsed due to the financial crisis caused by Brüning's lack of spending. In May the following year, Brüning resigned as chancellor.	
Hindenburg refused to make Hitler chancellor. In November, von Papen called another election, in which the Nazis won 196 seats.	
Hindenburg agreed to support this deal, as Hitler had the backing of large industrialists, landholders and the army. In January 1933, Adolf Hitler became chancellor of Germany.	

13 Explain two messages that were being presented to the public through Nazi propaganda.

....

....

14 The following statements describe the role of either Adolf Hitler or Joseph Goebbels in getting the Nazis into power. Tick the correct name for each statement.

Role	Hitler	Goebbels
He created a simple message, which could be repeated in various media formats.		
He helped to create the 25-Point Programme to offer something different to voters.		
He ensured that there were mass rallies in five cities during the 1932 presidential election.		
His speeches attracted many people and helped increased membership of the party.		
He was elected to the Reichstag in 1928.		
He presented a charismatic philosophy that all could understand, combined with a vision of making Germany the strongest nation in the world.		
He was appointed Minister for Propaganda and Popular Enlightenment in 1933.		

Exam-style questions

Section B

15 a Study Interpretations 3 and 4, which provide differing views regarding the Nazi Party's rise to power. What is the main difference between these views? Explain your answer, using details from both interpretations. **4 marks**

Interpretation 3

By October 1932, Hitler had the rare experience of speaking in a half-empty auditorium during a visit to Nuremberg, centre of the Nazi Franconian heartland. This critical period for Hitler indicates how dependent the manufactured Hitler 'charisma' was on conjunctural factors, how fragile it could be, and how only recurring success could guarantee its vitality.

From *The 'Hitler Myth'* (I. Kershaw, 1987)

Interpretation 4

To all the millions of discontented Hitler...offered what seemed to them, in their misery, some measure of hope. He would make Germany strong again, refuse to pay reparations, repudiate the Versailles Treaty, stamp out corruption, bring the money barons to heel (especially if they were Jews) and see to it that every German had a job and bread.

From *The Rise and Fall of the Third Reich: A History of Nazi Germany* (W. Shirer, 1960)

Hitler's rise to power, 1919–33

b Suggest one reason why Interpretations 3 and 4 give different views regarding the Nazi Party's rise to power.

(5 minutes, 4 marks)

c How far do you agree with Interpretation 4 about the Nazi Party's rise to power? Explain your answer, using both interpretations and your knowledge of the historical context. If you run out of space, you may continue your answer on a separate piece of paper.

(30 minutes, 20 marks)

How Hitler became chancellor of Germany, 1932–33

16 What event allowed Hitler to use emergency powers under Article 48?

17 Name the three chancellors that preceded Hitler and briefly state why each failed to stabilise the Weimar Republic between 1932 and 1933.

18 Describe two reasons for growth in Nazi electoral success between 1930 and 1933.

19 Describe the Wall Street Crash in no more than ten words.

20 Create a spider diagram to explain how each of the following events allowed Hitler to become chancellor by January 1933.

| Wall Street Crash | Electoral success, 1929–33 | Hitler's personal skill | Political instability, 1932–33 | Financial support for the Nazis |

21 Why was Hitler able to become chancellor in January 1933? Arrange the following nine factors (a–i) in the diamond nine template below. Put the most important at the top and work down to the least important at the bottom. There is no single correct answer, but you should be prepared to explain and justify your choices — do this in the space provided below the template.

- a Oratory
- b Propaganda
- c Economic depression caused by the Wall Street Crash
- d Failure of the Munich Putsch
- e 1932 election result
- f The Nazi Party's 25-Point Programme
- g Hatred of the Treaty of Versailles and the stab-in-the-back theory
- h Weak government (both constitution and democracy)
- i Financial support from big business

Exam-style questions

Section A

22 Explain why financial support helped the Nazi Party rise to power in January 1933.

You may use the following in your answer:

- the industrialists
- the Sturmabteilung (SA), otherwise known as the Brownshirts

You **must** also use information of your own. If you run out of space, you may continue your answer on a separate piece of paper.

(15) **12 marks**

Section B

23 Study Sources G and H. How useful are these sources for an enquiry into Hitler's rise to power?

Explain your answer using Sources G and H and your own knowledge of the historical context. If you run out of space, you may continue on a separate piece of paper.

8 marks

Source G

'Our last hope — Hitler'

Source H

Political party	Number of Reichstag seats	% of vote
Nazis (NSDAP)	230	37.4
Social Democrats (SDP)	133	21.6
Communist Party (KPD)	89	14.3
Centre Party (ZP)	75	12.5
National Party (DNVP)	37	5.9
People's Party (DVP)	7	1.2
Democratic Party (DDP)	4	1.0

Results of the July 1932 general election

Nazi control and dictatorship, 1933–39

The creation of a dictatorship, 1933–34

1. **Describe two ways that Hitler was able to deal with opposition after he claimed power in January 1933.**

   ....

   ....

2. **Explain how the Night of the Long Knives led to Hitler becoming Führer by August 1934.**

   ....

   ....

   ....

3. **Which statements are true and which are false? Circle True or False accordingly. Correct the false statements in the space provided below so that they are historically accurate.**

Statement	True/False?
In January 1933, Hitler's position as chancellor was not strong, as the Nazis did not have a majority in the Reichstag.	True/False
Herman van der Lubbe was a French Communist who was found at the scene of the Reichstag fire.	True/False
Following the fire, Hitler persuaded Hindenburg to sign the Decree for the Enablement of Protection, suspending civil rights.	True/False
The Nazi Party won 288 seats in the March 1933 election.	True/False
Despite increasing their vote share, the Nazis still did not win a majority. Therefore a coalition government was formed with the Centre Party.	True/False

   ....

   ....

   ....

   ....

4. **Put these events in chronological order by writing one of the numbers 1–7 in the empty column, with 1 being the earliest and 7 the latest.**

Event	Chronological order (1–7)
Night of the Long Knives	
Enabling Act	
Hitler becomes chancellor	
Trade unions banned	
The Nazi Party wins 288 seats in the general election	
Reichstag fire	
President Hindenburg's death	

5 Choose one of the events listed in Question 4 and explain how it helped Hitler to become a dictator.

....

....

....

....

6 Which of the following statements are causes, immediate consequences or long-term consequences of the Night of the Long Knives (1934)? Circle the answer accordingly.

Statement	Cause, immediate consequence or long-term consequence?
The SA were removed as a threat and the army offered its support to Hitler.	Cause Immediate consequence Long-term consequence
On 30 June 1934, Ernst Röhm and the main leaders of the SA were invited to a meeting. There they were executed by members of the SS (Röhm on 1 July).	Cause Immediate consequence Long-term consequence
Hitler gained confidence due to the lack of opposition to him consolidating power. A law was passed on 3 July 1934, which stated that Hitler's actions were legal.	Cause Immediate consequence Long-term consequence
The SA was made up of working-class men and led by Ernst Röhm, who believed in creating a socialist revolution.	Cause Immediate consequence Long-term consequence
Heinrich Himmler wanted Hitler's personal bodyguard, the SS, to break away from the SA and lead the armed forces.	Cause Immediate consequence Long-term consequence
Ernst Röhm wanted to incorporate the army into the SA in order to increase his power and limit an attack on the SA.	Cause Immediate consequence Long-term consequence
Opponents of Hitler, including the former chancellor Kurt von Schleicher and the politician Gregor Strasser, were killed.	Cause Immediate consequence Long-term consequence
In August 1934, with the death of President Hindenburg, the army swore an oath of loyalty to Hitler and he combined the posts of chancellor and president to become Führer.	Cause Immediate consequence Long-term consequence

Exam-style questions

Section B

7 a Study Interpretations 5 and 6, which provide differing views of the Reichstag fire. What is the main difference between these views? Explain your answer, using details from both interpretations.

Interpretation 5

Today there seems little doubt that it was precisely by allowing van der Lubbe to stand trial that the Nazis proved their innocence of the Reichstag fire. For had [he] been associated with them in any way, the Nazis would have shot him the moment he had done their dirty work, blaming his death on an outbreak of 'understandable popular indignation'.

From *The Reichstag Fire: Legend and Truth* (F. Tobias, 1963)

Interpretation 6

Rudolf Diels [head of the Political Police] wrote...to all police stations in Prussia: 'Communists reportedly plan to carry out systematic raids on police squads and members of nationalist associations with the aim of disarming them.'...'where necessary communist functionaries [are to be] placed under protective custody.'... *All* **of the fire experts agreed that the fire in the Reichstag...had to have been set by** *several* **culprits.**

From *The Reichstag Fire: How History is Created* (A. Bahar and W. Kugel, 2001)

b **Suggest one reason why Interpretations 5 and 6 give differing views regarding the impact of the Reichstag fire.**

[4 marks]

c How far do you agree with Interpretation 6 about the Reichstag fire? Explain your answer, using both interpretations and your knowledge of the historical context.

Make notes in the space below, then write your answer on a separate piece of paper.

⏱ 30   **20 marks**

The police state and control

8 The following key words relate to the Nazi state. In the final column, insert the correct letter, linking each key word to the correct definition.

Key word	Definition	Answer
a Aryan	Hitler's personal bodyguard and a powerful security and surveillance agency of the Nazi regime	
b Gestapo	An intelligence organisation designed to seek out potential threats to the state	
c SD	An agreement made between Hitler and the Pope not to interfere with the Catholic Church	
d SS	A resistance group of young people who listened to swing music and wrote anti-Nazi slogans on walls	
e Gleichschaltung	Set up to replace Christian values with pagan ideas and values	
f Concordat	The secret state police, used to monitor and apprehend opponents of the state	
g German Faith Movement	The process of controlling all aspects of German society, from education and the courts to the arts	
h Edelweiss Pirates	The word used to describe the Nazi ideal racial type	

9 In the table below, add both the date that each branch of authority within the police state was set up and the name of the person in charge.

Branch of authority	Date it was set up	Person in charge
SD		
SS		
Gestapo		
Concentration camps		

10 Briefly explain how the Nazi Party took over the legal system by 1936.

....

....

....

11 Sort the following statements into two columns in the table provided below: those policies associated with the Christian Church and those associated with the German Faith Movement.

Only 5% of the German population supported it.	Based on the teachings of the Bible.	Saw Hitler as a god-like figure.	Supported the Centre Party.
Owed its allegiance to the Pope.	The sun was an important symbol, as it represented a cross and links to ancient civilisations.	Taught love and forgiveness as values.	Believed in racial superiority.

Christian Church	German Faith Movement

12 The infiltration of the arts was another feature of control under the Nazi regime. Create a spider diagram to explain how each of the following art forms changed under Nazi rule.

Music	Theatre	Art	Sport	Architecture

Nazi control and dictatorship, 1933–39

13 Which statements are true and which are false? Circle True or False accordingly. Correct the false statements in the space provided below so that they are historically accurate.

Statement	True/False?
The SD originally ran the concentration camps.	True/False
The first concentration camp was built at Sachsenhausen in 1933.	True/False
The German Lawyers Front was established in October 1936.	True/False
Pope Pius XI signed a Concordat with Hitler in July 1933.	True/False
The Church's new national bishop was called Ludwig Müller.	True/False
Antisemitic signs were still present during the 1936 Olympic Games in Berlin.	True/False
Germany won fewer medals than any other nation at the 1936 Olympic Games in Berlin.	True/False

....

....

....

....

Exam-style questions

Section B

14 Study Sources I and J. How useful are these sources for an enquiry into Hitler's consolidation of power?

Explain your answer using Sources I and J and your own knowledge of the historical context. If you run out of space, you may continue on a separate piece of paper.

Source I

'We'll soon make you talk, you dog!'

The unfortunate scholar [was] beaten almost unconscious.

'Will you confess now?'

[The man] was alone with God. Praying, he awaited the shot that would put an end to his life.

The man's profound faith touched his tormentors. ... The SA men considered the situation. They conferred... The 'examination' came to an end. They [let the man go].
First-hand account from 17 May 1933

Source J

Decree of Appointment of Chief of Police:

I. In order to have the police functions in the Reich placed on a unified and centralized basis, a Chief of German Police is being appointed within the Reich Ministry of the Interior who will simultaneously be entrusted with the direction and handling of all police functions within the jurisdiction of the Ministry of the Interior of the Reich and Prussia.
Decree of 17 June 1936 concerning the appointment of the Chief of German Police

....

....

Section A

15 Give two points you can infer from Source K about the role of the Gestapo. Then add the details from the source that tell you this.

4 marks

Source K

People were always coming and saying 'Why haven't you hung out a flag for Hitler's birthday?' and so on...You almost went to jail. It was very dangerous if you didn't do it...Finally my mother bought a real tiny one.

A woman speaking in 1993 about the fear the Gestapo created

What I can infer:

....

....

Details in the source that tell me this:

....

....

....

What I can infer:

....

....

Details in the source that tell me this:

....

....

....

Opposition, resistance and conformity

16 a How successful were forms of resistance and opposition to the Nazi regime? Place the following five groups along the continuum in the table provided below, with the most successful form of opposition in the first column and the least successful in the final column.

| 1938 army generals' plot | Edelweiss Pirates | Protestant Church | Catholic Church | White Rose |

Most successful				Least successful

b Explain your choices.

....
....
....
....
....
....

17 a Write down five words to describe the Edelweiss Pirates.

....

b Write down five words to describe the Swing Youth.

....

c Complete the sentence:

The most successful resistance movement was .... because........................

....
....
....

18 Put the following measures of control into chronological order. Write one of the numbers 1–6 in the empty column, with 1 being the earliest and 6 the latest.

Measures	Chronological order (1–6)
The Nazis censored the Catholic press and harassed priests.	
1,600 newspapers and magazines were closed down.	
The Nazis removed the cross and crucifix from Catholic schools.	
Students in Berlin burnt 20,000 books written by Jewish, communist or anti-Nazi university professors.	
Hitler removed the generals who had criticised his foreign aims.	
70% of German families now owned a radio. The Nazi message was now transmitted directly into their homes.	

19 Which statements are true and which are false? Circle True or False accordingly. Correct the false statements in the space provided below so that they are historically accurate.

Statement	True/False?
There were three attempts to assassinate Hitler before 1939.	True/False
Swing boys often grew their hair long and girls wore brightly coloured make-up.	True/False
Pastor Martin Niemöller was a German Catholic who opposed the Nazi regime.	True/False
Army leaders set aside plans to overthrow Hitler after the Führer successfully conquered Poland.	True/False
Sophie Scholl was a member of the Red Rose Movement.	True/False
The Edelweiss Pirates were not considered a threat before 1939.	True/False

....
....
....
....

20 Which was more successful in controlling the population of Germany: propaganda or fear? Explain your answer.

....
....
....
....
....
....
....
....
....
....

21 Summarise Nazi control into an acrostic using the following word:

C ....
O ....
N ....
T ....
R ....
O ....
L ....

Exam-style questions

Section B

22 Study Sources L and M. How useful are these sources for an enquiry into the concentration camp system?

Explain your answer using Sources L and M and your own knowledge of the historical context. If you run out of space, you may continue on a separate piece of paper.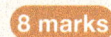

Source L

In normal occupancy, each barrack had 146 prisoners. This was true until mid-1938. After that, a third bed was added. Then the barrack occupancy was 180–200 men... In other barracks, the overcrowding of the camp led to the beds being removed and the straw sacks were laid on the ground.

Harry Naujoks, a survivor of Sachsenhausen concentration camp, recalling his experience in his book *My Life in Sachsenhausen Concentration Camp, 1936–42* (1987)

Source M

The Labour Service at Oranienburg concentration camp, 1933

Section A

23 Study Source N. Give two points you can infer from the source regarding the power of opposition in Nazi Germany. Then add the details from the source that tell you this.

⏱ 5 **4 marks**

Source N

Everyone has the right to an honest and workable government which guarantees the freedom of the individual and ensures the property of all... Our present 'state' is a dictatorship of evil... Why do you not rise up...? Sabotage armaments and war industry plants, meetings, festivals, organisations, anything which National Socialism has created. Hinder the smooth operation of the war machine.

Extract from a White Rose leaflet, 1943

What I can infer:

....
....

Details in the source that tell me this:

....
....
....
....

What I can infer:

....
....

Details in the source that tell me this:

....
....
....
....
....

Life in Nazi Germany, 1933–39

Nazi policies towards women and the young

1 Divide the following statements into two categories: those that describe the role of women in the 1920s and those that describe their role under the Nazi regime.

  a There were 100,000 women teachers and 3,000 doctors.
  b Women were encouraged to be healthy and wear their hair in a bun.
  c Divorce was permitted if a husband or wife was unable to have children.
  d Women could wear short skirts and make-up, and cut their hair short.
  e The government issued young couples with loans to help them marry, so long as the woman gave up her job.
  f One-tenth of the members of the Reichstag were women.
  g The number of women working increased from 11.6 million to 14.6 million because of male conscription into the armed forces.
  h Medals were awarded on Hitler's mother's birthday to women with large families.
  i Women went out unescorted and drank and smoked in public.
  j Women's organisations were established to promote household tasks and motherhood skills.
  k Those women who worked in the civil service earned the same wages as men.

Women in the 1920s	Women under the Nazi regime

2 Write down five words to describe the ideal image of a woman according to Nazi beliefs.

....

....

3 When the government took control of education, children had to attend school from ages six to fourteen and boys and girls were separated. Using the key words below, create a spider diagram to explain how each strand of the education system was changed to suit Nazi beliefs.

Teachers	Lessons	The curriculum	Textbooks	Youth groups

4 a When was the Hitler Youth set up?

....

b At what age did members join the Hitler Youth?

....

c What activities did its members take part in?

....

....

....

5 a When was the League of German Girls set up?

....

b At what age did members join the League of German Girls?

....

c What activities did its members take part in?

....

....

....

6 Describe two methods employed by the Nazis to indoctrinate children.

....

....

....

....

7 Which statements are true and which are false? Circle True or False accordingly. Correct the false statements in the space provided below so that they are historically accurate.

Statement	True/False?
All school lessons began and ended with the students saluting and saying 'Heil Hitler'.	True/False
Youth organisations like the Edelweiss Pirates were ignored.	True/False
Most German women accepted the changes in society and returned to being homemakers.	True/False
Divorce was allowed and it contributed to a rise in the divorce rate by 1939.	True/False
The Little Fellows was the youngest version of the Hitler Youth.	True/False
The three Ks stood for children, church and home.	True/False

....

....

....

....

....

Life in Nazi Germany, 1933–39

Exam-style questions

Section B

8 a Study Interpretations 7 and 8, which provide differing views regarding Nazi policies. What is the main difference between these views? Explain your answer, using details from both interpretations.

(5) 4 marks

Interpretation 7

Hitler...lost no time in making plain to the cabinet that military spending was to be given absolute priority. During a discussion in cabinet on 8 February [1933] on the financial implications of building a dam in Upper Silesia, he intervened to tell his... colleagues that 'the next 5 years must be devoted to the restoration of the defence capacity of the German people'.

From *Hitler* (I. Kershaw, 2008)

Interpretation 8

Before the years of militaristic triumph, there were the years of a seemingly miraculous economic recovery. Gone were the strikes. Gone were the unemployment queues. The miracle had been accomplished by vast schemes of public works, the building of the motorways (Autobahnen), the improvement of the nation's infrastructure, and by putting Germany on a war economy...

From *Hitler: A Short Biography* (A. N. Wilson, 2012)

b Suggest one reason why Interpretations 7 and 8 give differing views on economic recovery in Nazi Germany.

(5) 4 marks

c How far do you agree with Interpretation 8 about economic changes in Nazi Germany? Explain your answer, using both interpretations and your knowledge of the historical context.

Make notes in the space below, then write your answer on a separate piece of paper.

⏱ 30 **20 marks**

Employment and living standards

9 The following key words relate to employment. In the final column, insert the correct letter, linking each key word to the correct definition.

Key word	Definition	Answer
a Rearmament	Compulsory enlistment of men into the armed forces.	
b The Reich Labour Service	The name of a one-pot dish comprising meat and vegetables.	
c Conscription	The process of building up military weapons.	
d Strength through Joy	The National Socialist trade union organisation that replaced all independent trade unions.	
e Eintopf	An organisation set up to provide young men with manual labouring jobs.	
f The German Labour Front	An organisation set up by the German Labour Front to provide leisure activities for workers.	

Life in Nazi Germany, 1933–39

41

10 How useful were the policies the Nazis introduced in order to reduce unemployment? Arrange the following terms along a continuum line, from least useful in the first column to most useful in the final column.

The Reich Labour Service	Job creation schemes	Invisible unemployment	Rearmament	Strength through Joy

Least useful				Most useful

11 Divide the following statements into two categories: those that show German people were better off under the new employment schemes and those that show they were not better off.

    a   Beauty of Labour was set up to improve working conditions. It installed better lighting in the workplace and improved noise levels for workers.

    b   Average weekly wages increased from 86 marks in 1932 to 109 marks in 1938.

    c   The Volkswagen car scheme encouraged workers to put money aside to purchase a car. By 1939 not a single person had taken delivery of a vehicle.

    d   Food items were in short supply and the cost of living increased because the government reduced agricultural output in order to protect farmers.

    e   Trade unions were banned and workers were prohibited from negotiating better pay or reduced hours.

    f   Strength through Joy improved leisure time for German workers by providing sports activities, trips, holidays and cruises. More than 10 million people took up the offer of these new holidays.

Better off	Not better off

12 To what extent did things improve for German workers?

....

....

....

....

....

13 a Describe Strength through Joy in five words.

....

....

    b Describe the Reich Labour Service in five words.

....

....

14 For what reason did Hitler make changes to German society? Arrange the following nine factors (a–i) in the diamond nine template below. Put the most important at the top and work down to the least important at the bottom. There is no single correct answer, but you should be prepared to explain and justify your choices — do this in the space provided below the template.

- a In preparation for war
- b To return Germany to a more 'traditional' path
- c To restore the economy
- d To improve citizens' lives
- e To reverse the actions of the Treaty of Versailles
- f To indoctrinate young people
- g To control the population
- h To make Germany a modern society
- i To 'racially purify' Germany

← most important

← least important

Exam-style questions

Section A

15 Give two points you can infer from Source O regarding Strength through Joy and Nazi beliefs. Then add the details from the source that tell you this.

⏱ 5   **4 marks**

Source O

What I can infer:

Your Volkswagen, poster from the 1930s

Details in the source that tell me this:

....
....
....

What I can infer:

....
....

Details in the source that tell me this:

....
....
....
....

Section A

16 Explain why Germans were better off in employment under Nazi rule.

You may use the following in your answer:
- Strength through Joy
- Beauty of Labour

You **must** also use information of your own. If you run out of space, you may continue your answer on a separate piece of paper.

⏱ 15   **12 marks**

The persecution of minorities

17 a From the moment the Nazi party took power they began to discriminate against and then persecute minority groups. Put these measures against Jewish people in chronological order by writing one of the numbers 1–6 in the empty column, with 1 being the earliest and 6 the latest.

Measure	Chronological order (1–6)
Kristallnacht	
Books written by Jewish authors were burnt	
The Nuremberg Laws	
The SA organised a boycott of shops and businesses owned by Jewish people	
There was a deliberate lull in the anti-Jewish campaign due to the Olympic Games	
Jewish people had a red letter 'J' added to their passports	

b Can you explain the ways in which the measures changed over time?

....
....
....
....
....
....
....
....

18 The following key words relate to the persecution of Jewish people in Nazi Germany. In the final column, insert the correct letter, linking each key word to the correct definition.

Key word	Definition	Answer
a Master race	To treat somebody differently based on race, religion or political belief	
b Subhuman	A surgical procedure used to prevent somebody from having children	
c Euthanasia	To refuse to buy goods from a shop or other business as a form of protest or punishment	
d Sterilisation	German phrase meaning people's community	
e Volksgemeinschaft	Nazi ideological belief which stated that the German people were a superior race	
f Persecution	Night of Broken Glass	
g Discrimination	A lower order of human being — the Nazis used this term as a label for those they considered 'degenerates'	
h Boycott	A term the Nazis used to describe Eastern Europeans including Russian and Polish peoples	
i Kristallnacht	The persistent ill treatment of a group of people based on their race or religion, or political oppression over a long period of time	
j Slavs	Killing by means of assisted suicide	

19 Which of the following statements are causes, immediate consequences or long-term consequences of Kristallnacht (1938)? Circle the answer accordingly.

Statement	Cause, immediate consequence or long-term consequence?
Goebbels portrayed the attacks on Jewish shops, business and synagogues as a spontaneous act of vengeance by Germans.	Cause / Immediate consequence / Long-term consequence
100 Jewish people were killed and 20,000 sent to concentration camps after the event. Goebbels organised anti-Jewish demonstrations, which soon involved attacks on Jewish shops, homes and synagogues.	Cause / Immediate consequence / Long-term consequence
The attacks began on the night of 9–10 November. So many shop windows were shattered that the event became known as the Night of Broken Glass (Kristallnacht).	Cause / Immediate consequence / Long-term consequence
Persecution continued into 1939. Jewish people were evicted from their homes and jewels and precious metals were confiscated.	Cause / Immediate consequence / Long-term consequence
The Anschluss with Austria made more Germans keen to remove 'non-Germans' from their country.	Cause / Immediate consequence / Long-term consequence
After the Olympic Games were over persecution quickly increased within Germany.	Cause / Immediate consequence / Long-term consequence
191 synagogues and 185 businesses were destroyed.	Cause / Immediate consequence / Long-term consequence
The Nazis banned Jewish people from owning or managing a business.	Cause / Immediate consequence / Long-term consequence
Herschel Grynszpan, a young Polish Jewish person, shot the German diplomat Ernst vom Rath in Paris.	Cause / Immediate consequence / Long-term consequence

20 a Explain the euthanasia campaign.

....

....

....

....

b Explain the Nazis' 'master race' belief.

....

....

....

....

21 Write down five words Nazis might have used to describe gypsies and gay people to justify sending them to concentration camps.

....

....

22 In the table below match each statement to the year in which the action took place or began.

Action	Year
Opponents of the Nazis were first sent to concentration camps.	1939
The mentally ill were secretly killed during the euthanasia programme.	1935
The Nazis banned all marriages between gypsies and Germans.	1938
Jewish shops and businesses were destroyed and Jewish people were made to pay for the damage.	1938
Jewish children were expelled from German schools.	1933
An organised boycott of Jewish shops and businesses took place for one day.	From 1935
Jewish people were no longer drafted into the German army.	1935
The Nuremberg Laws eliminated Jewish people's status as German citizens.	1933

Exam-style questions

Section B

23 a Study Interpretations 9 and 10, which provide differing views regarding the Nuremberg Laws. What is the main difference between these views? Explain your answer, using details from both interpretations.

4 marks

Interpretation 9

For Hitler, the aim remained the limitation of Jewish influence within Germany and the separation of the Jews from the body of the nation… Economic measures would be the next stage, but they must not create a situation that would turn the Jews into a public burden, thus carefully calculated steps were needed.

From *Nazi Germany and the Jews: The Years of Persecution 1933–39* (S. Friedlander, 1998)

Interpretation 10

Many ordinary Germans did not overly concern themselves with measures taken against the Jews. What mattered more to them was the massive reduction in unemployment that had occurred since Hitler came to power — from 6 million unemployed in 1933 to fewer than 2 million by 1936.

From *The Holocaust: A New History* (L. Rees, 2017)

b Suggest one reason why Interpretations 9 and 10 give different views regarding the purpose of the Nuremberg Laws.

⏱ 5   **4 marks**

....
....
....

c How far do you agree with Interpretation 10's stance on the Nuremberg Laws? Explain your answer, using both interpretations and your knowledge of the historical context.

Make notes in the space below, then write your answer on a separate piece of paper.

⏱ 30   **20 marks**

....
....
....
....
....
....
....
....
....
....

Hodder Education, an Hachette UK company, Carmelite House, 50 Victoria Embankment, London, EC4Y 0DZ

Orders

Please contact Hachette UK Distribution, Hely Hutchinson Centre, Milton Road, Didcot, Oxfordshire, OX11 7HH

tel: 01235 827827

e-mail: education@hachette.co.uk

Lines are open 9.00 a.m.–5.00 p.m., Monday to Friday. You can also order through the Hodder Education website: www.hoddereducation.co.uk

© Philip Arkinstall 2018

ISBN 978-1-5104-1902-5

First printed 2018

The authorised representative in the EEA is Hachette Ireland, 8 Castlecourt Centre, Dublin 15, D15 XTP3, Ireland (email: info@hbgi.ie)

Impression number 7

Year 2022

All rights reserved; no part of this publication may be reproduced, stored in a retrieval system, or transmitted, in any form or by any means, electronic, mechanical, photocopying, recording or otherwise without either the prior written permission of Hodder Education or a licence permitting restricted copying in the United Kingdom issued by the Copyright Licensing Agency Ltd, www.cla.co.uk

Cover photo: Glasshouse Images/Alamy Stock Photo. Other photos used by permission of Photo 12/Contributor/Getty (p. 5), Keystone/Staff/Getty (p. 9), Heritage Images/Contributor/Getty (p. 17), Granger Historical Picture Archive/Alamy Stock Photo (p. 26), Mary Evans Picture Library/Imagno (p. 36), Shawshots/Alamy Stock Photo (p. 43)

Typeset by Aptara, India

Printed in the UK

Hachette UK's policy is to use papers that are natural, renewable and recyclable products and made from wood grown in well-managed forests and other controlled sources. The logging and manufacturing processes are expected to conform to the environmental regulations of the country of origin.

HODDER EDUCATION

t: 01235 827827
e: education@hachette.co.uk
w: hoddereducation.co.uk